I Thank God for You!

By Rose Duffy

For a FREE MP3 of my song, contact me at
www.RoseDuffyCreations.com
I will email this song to you!

Lyrics to *"I Thank God for You"*

I like to sing with you
I like to swim with you
I like to play in the park, jump in the leaves and look at the stars
I like to catch butterflies with you
Oh, how I thank God for you!

I like to bake with you
I like to eat cake with you
I like to ride in the car, play hide-and-seek and catch with the ball
I like to dance in the rain with you
Oh, how I thank God for you!

I like to clap with you
I like to laugh with you
I like to make funny faces, color our pictures and visit new places
I like to run really fast with you
Oh, how I thank God for you!

And now it's time for me to sleep
So tomorrow I'll have energy
But I never … I never, ever, ever fall asleep
Before I thank God for You

Written and sung by Rose Duffy
Music and production by Scottie Miller
Engineered, mixed and mastered by Steve Kaul. Wild Sound Recording Studio,
Minneapolis, Minnesota

ABOUT THIS BOOK

I Thank God for You is a bedtime ritual which helps tuck our little ones into bed with that "feel-good" feeling. *I Thank God for You* is a small book, jam-packed with the following messages that are so important to instill into the hearts and minds of our loved ones at a very young age:

* Love
* Gratitude
* Forgiveness
* Confidence
* Faith in God
* Value (every little thing they do has special meaning)
* Humor
* Appreciation for the small things in life

These messages are crucial in establishing and building upon a strong, solid foundation for today's young kids. No doubt your little one(s) will always remember going through the motions of this book together with you as a bedtime ritual.

I wrote *I Thank God for You* several years ago when my now-grown kids were little. I never stopped believing in the value of it—not only for children but for parents as well. It's a reminder for parents to take a step back in this fast-paced world and enjoy and love their children in the most treasurable and memorable ways. I'm convinced it's the simple things that stay with our kids well into adulthood.

Please contact me through my website at www.RoseDuffyCreations.com in order to receive a free MP3 of my song which goes along with this book. It is my hope that you will sing this song together with your kid(s). In doing so, you and your kid(s) will never, ever, fall asleep before thanking God for one another.

ROSE DUFFY is a tenor saxophonist, flute player and songwriter from the Twin Cities. She knows enough about the piano to help write songs such as "I Thank God for You." This is Rose's first book. At 60 years old, Rose is full proof it's never too late to follow your passion and purpose in life.

ACKNOWLEDGEMENTS

I'd like to thank my friend Susan Hughes for her proofreading and editing skills. Susan, you are a gem! I'd also like to thank my musician friend Scottie Miller (on piano and production) and my studio engineer friend, Steve Kaul of Wild Sound Recording Studio. You both gave it your all on a project you quickly recognized as being very important to me. I would also like to acknowledge my two biggest cheerleaders, Penny Ranan and Deborah Hartung. I could always count on you for your enthusiasm and for your opinions. To John ElHanafi, a friend whom I've never even met in person, thank you for your ongoing help with my website for no other reason than believing in me. A big shout-out goes to Brian Del Turco for his spot-on formatting skills and final touches in pulling everything together. Last, but surely not least, I am grateful to all of you who have purchased my work. God bless all of you.

Sincerely,

Rose Duffy

To my adult kids, Carly, Kevin, and Jason: You continue to tuck me into bed every night, whether near or far.

I thank God for you!

Love,
Mom

1998   2019

I Thank God for You!

"It's time for bed, little one. Let's lie down together for a little while, and then I'll tuck you in for the night."

I Thank God for You!

"Mommy, who tucks you in at night?"

"In a very magical way, you do."

"How does that work, Mommy? You always tuck me in for the night."

"Sometimes we get a little angry with each other, right?"

"Sometimes."

I Thank God for You!

"Well, I take my blanket, and I shake that anger away ... just like this."

I Thank God for You!

"Then I remember something very special, so I set my blanket down on my ankles ... just like this."

I Thank God for You!

"I think about those pretty yellow flowers you like to surprise me with."

I Thank God for You!

"The ones you put in your purple vase, Mommy?"

"Yes! They always warm my heart. I thank God for you."

I Thank God for You!

"Then I start to pull my blanket up a little bit more ... and I remember something very special, so I set my blanket down on my knees ... just like this. Remember those silly faces you always make?"

"Like this?"

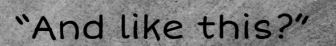
"And like this?"

I Thank God for You!

"Yes, just like that! Your silly faces always make me laugh! I thank God for you."

I Thank God for You!

"Then I start to pull my blanket up a little bit more ... and I remember something very special, so I set my blanket down on my tummy ... just like this."

I Thank God for You!

"I like to think about those beautiful pictures you draw."

I Thank God for You!

"The ones you put on our refrigerator, Mommy?"

"Yes. They always make me smile! I thank God for you."

I Thank God for You!

"Then I start to pull my blanket up a little bit more ... and I remember something very special, so I set my blanket right on my heart ... just like this."

I Thank God for You!

"Remember how you always tell me that I'm the best mommy in the whole entire world?"

"Yes, because you are the best mommy in the whole entire world!"

"Well, that makes me feel very proud! I thank God for you."

I Thank God for You!

"Then I start to pull my blanket up just a little bit more ... and I snuggle it up to my neck ... just like this."

I Thank God for You!

"I lie down ... I close my eyes ... I think about you ... I feel the magic ... and I thank God for you."

I Thank God for You!

"And now it's time for you to sleep. Good night, little one."

"Good night. I thank God for you too, Mommy!"

56197320R00027

Made in the USA
Columbia, SC
22 April 2019